D0578116

COLORADO

A PHOTOGRAPHIC PORTFOLIO

CARR CLIFTON
Maroon Bells and Maroon Bells Lake,
Maroon Bells/Snowmass Wilderness, White River National Forest

COLORADO

A PHOTOGRAPHIC PORTFOLIO

BROWNTROUT PUBLISHERS, INC.
SAN FRANCISCO

WILLARD CLAY
Monkey flower along Fraser Creek,
White River National Forest, Flat Tops Wilderness

COLORADO: A PHOTOGRAPHIC PORTFOLIO
features the finest photographs of Colorado by a
distinguished group of landscape photographers. Captions
for the photographs were provided by the photographers.

Photographs, Captions © 1995
Denver A. Bryan, Willard Clay, Carr Clifton,
Kathleen Norris Cook, Terry Donnelly, Jack W. Dykinga,
Dennis Flaherty, Jeff Foott, Fred Hirschmann,
George H. H. Huey, Barbara Magnuson, David Muench,
Marc Muench, Steve Mulligan, James Randklev,
Galen Rowell/Mountain Light, Tom Till, Larry Ulrich

LIBRARY OF CONGRESS
CATALOGING-IN-PUBLICATION DATA

Colorado, a photographic portfolio.
    p.   cm.
   ISBN 1-56313-616-3 (hardcover : alk. paper)
   ISBN 1-56313-758-5 (softcover : alk. paper)
   1. Colorado—Pictorial works.
F777.C63 1995   95-18913
978.8—dc20   CIP

Printed and bound by
Dai Nippon Printing Company, Ltd., Hong Kong

10 9 8 7 6 5 4 3 2

THE PHOTOGRAPHS

DAVID MUENCH
Sunflowers, Great Sand Dunes National Monument

INTRODUCTION

THE landscape photographer in Colorado today is working within a grand tradition. Just as William Henry Jackson's photographs of the Yellowstone area in the 1860s led to the establishment of the world's first national park and Ansel Adams' and Eliot Porter's images of wilderness inspired the environmental movement of the middle twentieth century, the photographs in this book can affect the way that people see the natural world and can help build a new movement for its preservation.

Each of the artists included in this volume have themselves been changed by the awesome power of the photographic image. Most are established professionals whose work appears in all the appropriate commercial and artistic settings. Their restless wanderings often take

them to the heart of the Rocky Mountains of North America in Colorado where that mighty range reaches above 14,000 feet and looms over the western extension of the Great Plains. All would agree that Colorado affords them profoundly moving scenes which they take as their task to capture and interpret.

But the camera is a tool not merely of observation but also of creation. Where the tired or indifferent traveler sees only dust and the slanting light of afternoon, the sensitive observer combines these elements into a beautiful representation of the passage of time and the suspension of the earthbound in the formless air. Without the artist the moment slips unrecorded into the infinite void. Indeed, it can be claimed that in an artless world both time and

history dissolve into nothingness since there would be no medium to sustain those temporal delusions.

The grandeur of Colorado's natural landscape defies the writer's ability to describe it because the conventional store of adjectives and superlatives is inadequate to the task. The skilled and patient photographer, by contrast, can ally himself with the powers of nature itself. Given enough time, the moon will rise, the mist will clear, the shadows will climb the canyon walls. And each passing minute recreates the world in ways that no one could imagine. That is why photography done well is so surprising—it shows us what we have *not* seen before, even in places we have been all of our lives. This is the Colorado we have sought to portray in this book.

TERRY DONNELLY
Fresh snow on pines in the Collegiate Peaks Wilderness,
San Isabel National Forest

JACK DYKINGA
Lupine and Indian paintbrush flowering in meadow with aspens at dawn, Rio Grande National Forest

DAVID MUENCH
Huron Peak top, Collegiate Peaks Wilderness

DENVER BRYAN
Mule deer bucks

LARRY ULRICH
Lower Blue Lake from Blue Lakes Pass, Mt. Sneffels Wilderness,
Uncompahgre National Forest, San Juan Mountains

FRED HIRSCHMANN
Morning light illuminating monoliths and spires,
Colorado National Monument

KATHLEEN NORRIS COOK
San Juan Mountains near Corkscrew Pass

LARRY ULRICH
Sneezeweed, West Elk Mountains,
Gunnison National Forest

JACK W. DYKINGA
Prairie sunflowers on the dunes,
Great Sand Dunes National Monument

WILLARD CLAY
Sunset light on Longs Peak and Trail Ridge,
Rocky Mountain National Park

JACK W. DYKINGA
Fireweed in bloom, Grand Mesa National Forest

TOM TILL
Wet sand, Great Sand Dunes National Monument

CARR CLIFTON
Fall-colored aspens,
Maroon Bells/Snowmass Wilderness,
White River National Forest

LARRY ULRICH
Yellow pond lilies, Molas Divide,
San Juan National Forest

DAVID MUENCH
Sprague Lake sunrise,
Rocky Mountain National Park

TOM TILL
Evening, Monument Canyon, Colorado National Monument

TERRY DONNELLY
Sculpted rocks above the Lincoln Creek Grottos, White River National Forest

GEORGE H. H. HUEY
Sunset, Blue Mesa Lake,
Curecanti National Recreation Area

GEORGE H. H. HUEY
Rocky Mountain bee plant growing on the edge of the dunes,
Great Sand Dunes National Monument

DAVID MUENCH
Winter transition, snow carpet in Dallas Divide, southwest Colorado

DENVER A. BRYAN
Pronghorn antelope fawn, one day old and exhibiting "still behavior" to avoid danger

JACK W. DYKINGA
Aspens surround pond atop mesa,
Grand Mesa National Forest

BARBARA MAGNUSON
Mountain goat nannies running across ridge,
Mount Evans, Arapahoe National Forest

GEORGE H. H. HUEY
Prairie sunflower, Great Sand Dunes National Monument

CARR CLIFTON
Sun-glazed snow on Independence Pass

KATHLEEN NORRIS COOK
East Dallas Creek area, San Juan Mountains

CARR CLIFTON
Fresh snowfall on conifers along the Fryingpan River

DAVID MUENCH
Sierra Blanca, Rio Grande

CARR CLIFTON
Unnamed pass in the Maroon Bells/Snowmass Wilderness

KATHLEEN NORRIS COOK
Winter sky at Lizard Head Pass, San Juan Mountains

DAVID MUENCH
Bunch grass in San Luis Valley, Sangre de Cristo Range

46

MARC MUENCH
Uncompahgre National Forest, San Juan Mountains

GEORGE H. H. HUEY
Snakeweed and rabbitbrush, sunset, Great Sand Dunes National Monument,
Sangre de Cristo Mountains in background

JACK W. DYKINGA
Primrose and spruce against cascading streams in Chicago Basin,
San Juan National Forest

LARRY ULRICH
Aspens and Wolcott Mountain from Dallas Divide,
San Juan Mountains

DAVID MUENCH
Uncompahgre River Canyon,
Sneffels Range

DENNIS FLAHERTY
The Coke Ovens at sunrise,
Colorado National Monument

MARC MUENCH
Continental Divide from Trail Ridge, Rocky Mountain National Park

CARR CLIFTON
Fireweed and fleabane daisies,
Maroon Bells/Snowmass Wilderness

WILLARD CLAY
Winter scene below Lizard Head Peak,
San Juan National Forest

JEFF FOOTT
Bighorn sheep rams, rut behavior

DAVID MUENCH
Flagged bristlecone pines, Mosquito Range

JACK W. DYKINGA
(Preceding pages) Lupine and goldenpea flowering amid elk-scarred aspens,
Rio Grande National Forest

DAVID MUENCH
(Immediate preceding pages) Pawnee Buttes

Aspen trees, Maroon Bells/Snowmass Wilderness, White River National Forest

CARR CLIFTON
Aspen trees, Maroon Bells/Snowmass Wilderness, White River National Forest

CARR CLIFTON
Thunderclouds over Independence Lake, Hunter-Fryingpan Wilderness

FRED HIRSCHMANN
Warm light of dusk illuminating the Great Sand Dunes and Mount Herard of the Sangre de Cristo Mountains,
Great Sand Dunes National Monument

JACK DYKINGA
Mount Crested Butte and Gothic Mountain
at first light with fog on meadows with rain-soaked skyrockets,
Gunnison National Forest

TERRY DONNELLY
Scattered spring clouds over the Central Garden area, Garden of the Gods

JAMES RANDKLEV
Wildflowers carpet Yankee Boy Basin, San Juan Mountains

LARRY ULRICH
Aspens along the Big Thompson River, Morraine Park, Rocky Mountain National Park

DAVID MUENCH
Storm, Mount Taylor, Rocky Mountain National Park

TOM TILL
Sunset, Crestone Peak, Sangre de Cristo Mountains

DENVER A. BRYAN
Bobcat in brush in winter habitat

STEVE MULLIGAN
(Preceding) Twin Sisters, El Paso County

TOM TILL
North Clear Creek Falls, Rio Grande National Forest

TERRY DONNELLY
Aspen grove in snow, Clear Creek Canyon, San Isabel National Forest

DENVER A. BRYAN
Snowy owl perched on post in winter habitat

DAVID MUENCH
Above Stony Gulch, San Juan Mountains, Weminuche Wilderness

FRED HIRSCHMANN
(Preceding) Pinyon-juniper forest and sandstone cliffs,
Glade Park

CARR CLIFTON
Fall-colored aspens, Elk Mountains

WILLARD CLAY
Algae-covered beaver pond near Kebler Pass,
Gunnison National Forest

CARR CLIFTON
Ice and cottonwoods at sunset,
Curecanti National Recreation Area

MARC MUENCH
Uncompahgre National Forest, San Juan Mountains

DAVID MUENCH
Cumberland Basin, La Plata Mountains

JEFF FOOTT
Coyote, hunting mice

JAMES RANDKLEV
Summer thunderstorm and rainbow over Cascade Mountain,
Uncompahgre Primitive Area, San Juan Mountains

GALEN ROWELL
Bristlecone pine on Mount Evans (14,260 feet)

DAVID MUENCH
Canyon falls, Crystal River tributary, White River National Forest

MARC MUENCH
Independence Pass

FRED HIRSCHMANN
Spruce-fir forest among volcanic hoodoos,
Wheeler Geologic Area, La Garita Mountains, Rio Grande National Forest

DAVID MUENCH
*(Preceding) Snowmass Mountain,
Maroon Bells/Snowmass Wilderness*

MARC MUENCH
Wolf Creek Pass, San Juan National Forest

DAVID MUENCH
Summer skies, Pawnee Butte, Pawnee National Grasslands

DAVID MUENCH
Winter drifts, San Miguel Mountains

JACK W. DYKINGA
The Elk Mountains aglow at sunset with the start of a rainbow and meadows
of blue columbine, Gunnison National Forest

MARC MUENCH
Colorado National Monument

GEORGE H. H. HUEY
Medano Creek with sand from dunes and cottonwood trees,
Great Sand Dunes National Monument

DAVID MUENCH
Bristlecone pines, Mosquito Range